LITTLE BIOGRAPHIES OF BIG PEOPLE

ELIZABETH CADY STANTON

By Joan Stoltman

Gareth Stevens PUBLISHING

Please visit our website, www.garethstevens.com. For a free color catalog of all our high-quality books, call toll free 1-800-542-2595 or fax 1-877-542-2596.

Library of Congress Cataloging-in-Publication Data

Names: Stoltman, Joan, author.
Title: Elizabeth Cady Stanton / Joan Stoltman.
Description: New York : Gareth Stevens Publishing, [2019] | Series: Little biographies of big people | Includes index.
Identifiers: LCCN 2017061600| ISBN 9781538218365 (library bound) | ISBN 9781538218389 (pbk.) | ISBN 9781538218396 (6 pack)
Subjects: LCSH: Stanton, Elizabeth Cady, 1815-1902–Juvenile literature. | Feminists–United States–Biography–Juvenile literature. | Suffragists–United States–Biography–Juvenile literature. | Women's rights–United States–History–19th century–Juvenile literature. | Suffrage–United States–History–Juvenile literature.
Classification: LCC HQ1413.S67 S756 2019 | DDC 305.42092 [B] –dc23
LC record available at https://lccn.loc.gov/2017061600

Published in 2019 by
Gareth Stevens Publishing
111 East 14th Street, Suite 349
New York, NY 10003

Designer: Sarah Liddell
Editor: Kate Mikoley

Photo credits: series art Yulia Glam/Shutterstock.com; cover, p. 1 Universal History Archive/Contributor/Universal Images Group/Getty Images; p. 5 Historical/Contributor/Corbis Historical/Getty Images; p. 7 Fæ/Wikimedia Commons; p. 9 Time Life Pictures/Contributor/The LIFE Picture Collection/Getty Images; p. 11 (main) Epics/Contributor/Hulton Archive/Getty Images; pp. 11 (inset), 17 Bettmann/Contributor/Bettmann/Getty Images; p. 13 Scewing/Wikimedia Commons; p. 15 ullstein bild Dtl./Contributor/Getty Images; p. 19 Elisa.rolle/Wikimedia Commons; p. 21 AFP/Staff/AFP/Getty Images.

Printed in the United States of America

CPSIA compliance information: Batch #CS18GS: For further information contact Gareth Stevens, New York, New York at 1-800-542-2595.

CONTENTS

Boldface words appear in the glossary.

A Girl in a Man's World

Elizabeth Cady was born in 1815. As a child, she spent time in the law office where her father worked. There, she learned how few rights women had. Elizabeth wanted to cut out the pages of her father's books with laws that blocked women's rights.

An Excellent Education

Elizabeth worked hard in school. She was the only girl in the advanced math and languages classes during grade school. Elizabeth later went to Emma Willard's Troy Female Seminary, a special school for girls. There, she received the best education available for girls at the time.

A Fight for Rights

Elizabeth married Henry Brewster Stanton in 1840. He worked toward abolition, or an end to **slavery**. After their wedding, they went to the World Anti-Slavery **Convention**. At the convention, women didn't have the same rights as men. Elizabeth was **determined** to fight for women's rights.

A Movement Was Started

In 1848, Elizabeth helped put together the first ever women's rights convention. Around 300 people went to the meeting in Seneca Falls, New York. They talked about which laws they should work on changing first. Elizabeth pushed for women's suffrage, or the right to vote.

A Friend and Ally

In 1851, Elizabeth met Susan B. Anthony. They became a great team. Elizabeth wrote articles, **pamphlets**, and speeches from home while caring for her children. When Elizabeth's children were young, Susan traveled all over spreading Elizabeth's work.

SUSAN B. ANTHONY

Fighting Slavery

During the **American Civil War**, Elizabeth and Susan formed an abolition group. They got over 300,000 people to sign **petitions** that called to end slavery. After the war, they pushed for voting rights for everyone. However, only black men gained the right to vote.

Back to the Women's Movement

In 1866, Elizabeth became the first woman to run for Congress. In 1869, she and Susan started the National Woman Suffrage Association, a group that fought for voting rights. She wanted laws rewritten to include women! Elizabeth was president of the group for 20 years.

JOIN THE
NATIONAL
WOMAN'S
SUFFRAGE
ASSOCIATION
JOIN THE
NATIONAL
WOMENS
SUFFRAGE
ASSOCIATIO

Elizabeth worked for more than voting rights. Her work for **divorce**, fair pay, and more caused some groups to cast her out. But that didn't stop her! Having learned in childhood how important laws were, Elizabeth kept pushing for new laws and changes to old laws.

Never Afraid to Speak

Elizabeth fought for many years for women's suffrage. She died in 1902 and wasn't able to see women get the right to vote 18 years later. Still, Elizabeth helped bring about many important changes. You live in a better world today because of Elizabeth Cady Stanton!

"Truth is the only safe ground to stand upon."
—Elizabeth Cady Stanton

GLOSSARY

American Civil War: a war fought from 1861 to 1865 in the United States between the Union (the Northern states) and the Confederacy (the Southern states)

convention: a gathering of people who have a common interest or purpose

determined: having a strong feeling that you are going to do something and that you will not allow anyone or anything to stop you

divorce: the ending of a marriage by law

pamphlet: a small book that gives information

petition: a written request signed by many people

slavery: the state of being "owned" by another person and forced to work without pay

FOR MORE INFORMATION

BOOKS

Carson, Mary Kay. *Why Couldn't Susan B. Anthony Vote?: And Other Questions About . . . Women's Suffrage*. New York, NY: Sterling Children's Books, 2015.

Rappaport, Doreen. *Elizabeth Started All the Trouble*. New York, NY: Disney Hyperion, 2016.

WEBSITES

Biography: Elizabeth Cady Stanton
www.ducksters.com/history/civil_rights/elizabeth_cady_stanton.php
Learn more about Elizabeth Cady Stanton here.

Places Where Women Made History
www.nps.gov/nr/travel/pwwmh/womlist1.htm
Read about over 70 different places in New York and Massachusetts where women made a difference.

National Women's History Museum: Topics
nwhm.org/students-and-educators/topics
Choose from 16 topics to read about on the National Women's History Museum website.

INDEX